The Sigils

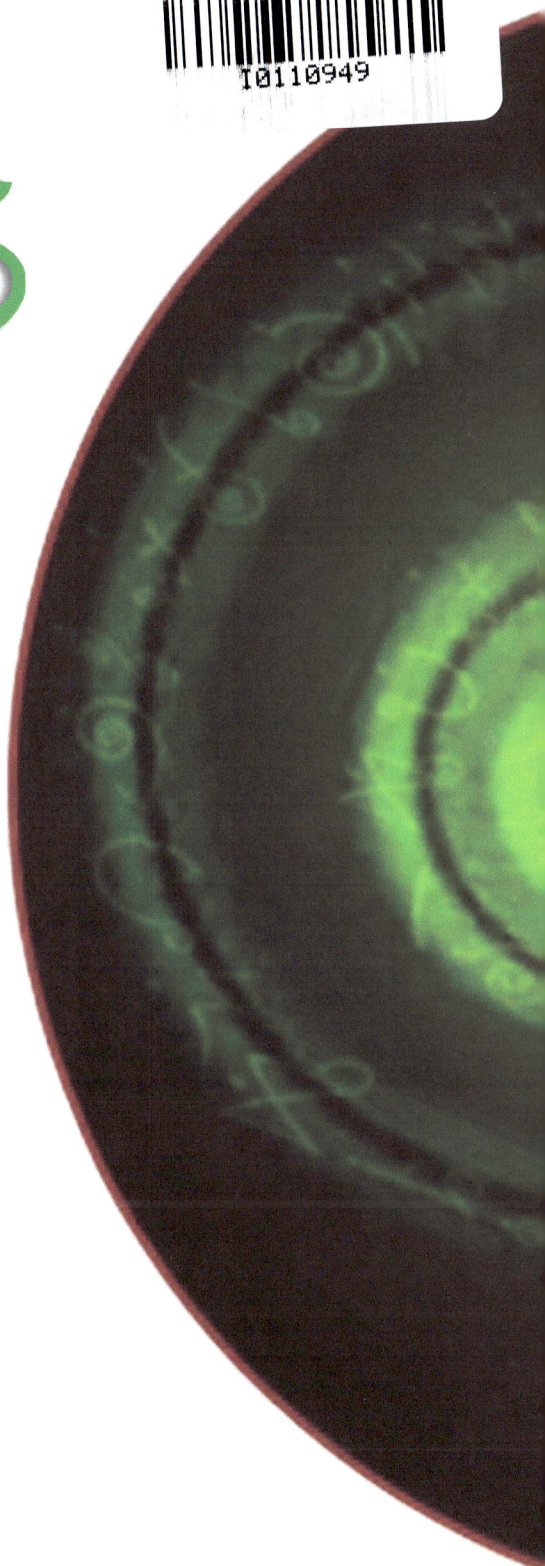

TREASURES

OF THE
FAERY COVENANT

A Green Fire Folio

By
Coleston Brown

Published in 2013 by

Le Brun Publications

Canada, Ireland

ISBN-13:   9780986591273

Cover art and design
by Coleston Brown
Book design by Coleston Brown

A Green Fire Folio on the
Faery Tradition

Contents

Acknowledgments

First and foremost, my heartfelt gratitude to those Faery companions with whom I live and walk and have my being each day. To Faery Artist Jessie Skillen, for much love & support, & for helpful advice on the design and selection of images, including several of her own inspired works I would also like to thank The members of the Spinners Group for initial guidance and support in vision.. Also particular thanks to Joann Alison, Katie Belle, Laurel Bohart, Gill Bourne, Alison Dias, Gill Finlayson, João Claudio Fuentes, Sara George, April Gorenflo, Anita Greg, Sue Kearley, Coleen Lane, Carol Reid, Caithleen Carter Steeves, Rab Wilkie, John Willmott, Bill Woodcock, and others unnamed for comments and assistance on the Sigil and Faery Covenant work in general. Many thanks also to Cliff and Pauline McClinton, and also to "Twilight and "the Pixie," for ongoing support and encouragement.

Preface

The Faery Sigils were first received by me in a Dream Vision done with a group of friends. in April 2010, which I give below:

> "I stood at the foot of a grassy hill. I saw a woman in green hooded tunic and red cloak, carrying a large shallow silver bowl. "Etain!" I thought and ran up the hill. She looked at me — a strange look of compassion and coldness combined — then knelt and set the bowl in a small depression in the earth. The bowl became a well and the golden birds on it's rim transformed into live birds and flew away. She gestured for me to kneel and look into the water. I saw a vision of turbulent dark clouds and lightning, heard the sound of hammer on anvil. Etain touched my hand (such a feeling!) and I saw it had turned red. I raised it to her, then placed it into the water—redness flowed from it and the clouds cleared revealing a blood red moon.
>
> "The moon filled the circle of the bowl/well. I recognised the shape of the rabbit or hare in the moon — so well-known in sacred lore throughout the world — and thought of the rabbits in the well near Tullyhogue.* Then the moon went through its waxing phase, until it disappeared into darkness and the void opened up. Strange signs and sigils began to swirl up and into my hand. "I don't know these" I said to Etain. She looked at me, and I knew the meanings of the signs were best not known yet. They were to be carried, and released in the course of life.
>
> "The new moon appeared in the well, a tiny sliver of bright light, the redness now gone. I watched it fill the well. Something flew up, which startled me and caused me to take my hand from the water ... It was a butterfly! It landed on my hand momentarily (the feeling was the same as Etain's touch), then flew off. I heard the songs and calls of birds, then the flutter of wings. I raised my hand to Etain, as the vision faded."

> April 17, 2010

At the time of this vision, I realised that the shapes I had been given to carry within me were the signs or sigils of the Faery Covenant. The Faery Covenant is an ancient binding agreement between Human and Faery Beings that arises out of the First Light, the primordial awareness in which all beings shared at the beginning of time. The Covenant is intimately bound up with our relations with the Faery, and hence with Nature, animals spiritual beings, Ancestors, each other and also with the Self. As such the Covenant is crucial for the fulfilment of Human destiny and the destiny of our planet.

---

* A friend had recently found dead rabbits in the well at Tullyhogue~ an ancient coronation site of the Irish Kings.

One day, soon after the above vision, I was idly doodling when I found myself rapidly drawing out a series of rune-like shapes, which I soon realised were the Sigils I'd seen in my Vision.

After further meditation and reflection, it eventually came to me that these shapes are not so much *a result* of the Faery Covenant, as they *are* the Faery Covenant. The Sigils encapsulate and express the essence of the Faery Covenant itself.

I realised that the sigil shapes were formed from a blending of iconic faery elements (spiral, thorn, stem, berry) and principles (reflection, reversal), and the Latin letter forms, which latter have roots in the ancient Phoenician alphabet that is the forebear of most of the world's alphabets (this includes the norse runic alphabet). This fusion of human & faery elements is both apropos and effective as an expression of the renewed Covenant between Faery and human that is currently coming into being from many different quarters and in many different forms today. There are 27 Sigils, corresponding to each of the 26 Latin letters plus one (The Thorn Sigil) that signifies a pause, a breath, or the space in between breaths.

In this Folio each sigil page opens with a few words on the general significance and meaning of the Sigil followed by sections headed:

i. ***Base position on the Faery Tree,*** indicating the relevant "path" or branch on the Tree of Faery,. The Faery Tree is not a new or different way of drawing the Magical Tree familiar to so many as the Tree of Life, so much as a different perspective on the dynamics of the Tree. Considerable benefit will be gained from consulting my folios on the Magical Tree and the Faery Tree.

ii. ***Important Star Forms,*** denoting the more significant planets and constellations that resonate with each sigil.

iii. ***Magical Applications,*** suggesting various ways of using the sigils for magical work.

iv. ***The Visionary Gateway,*** which is a brief visionary portal that is capable of opening up into deep, transformative vision of the presences and powers embodied and expressed through each sigil.

v. ***Oracular Meanings,*** which gives key words and a useful overview of the meaning of the Sigils when approached as an oracle or method of divining.

It is a great privilege to be able to present here this particular expression of the Faery Covenant and I hope to share to share other aspects in some of the forthcoming Green Fire Folios on the Faery Tradition.

CYH Brown, Carrowreagh, County Sligo, Éire— May, 2013

Ah (the A Sigil):
The Stag,
The Bird.

General significance: The Faery Sigil *Ah* holds a unique and important position, signifying both creative energy and the divine void; both original breath and creative pause. *Ah* is the great bridging power of Spirit. The sound of orgasm and breathing. The primal centre. There is thus some resonance between *Ah* and the Thorn Sigil (see page 32). *Ah* signifies the Faery Fool who carries all sigils and letters in his magic bundle.

The shape of *Ah* suggests a bird or a horned animal. Birds, and horned creatures appear often among the images and signs of the Old Stone Age. Such representations contain the first indications of human alphabets and scripts. But more importantly they signify a magical or symbolic mode of communication between human and Faery. *Ah* thus embodies and expresses all the sigils, in condensed magical form.

The predominance of the horned animal and the bird in the ancient rock paintings and scribings reflects both the centring of creative power and its flow between Worlds and Realms. Animals in Faery lore that are particularly associated with the Sigil *Ah* are the swan, eagle, bull, cow and stag.

Base Position on the Faery Tree: Branch 10-8.

As the most mobile of the faery sigils, embracing all the vowels and consonants, Like the letter A on the magical Tree, *Ah* moves freely about the Branches of the Faery Tree. One of its more important interchanges, is that it opens up the "Sphere of Destiny" model of the Tree, along with the Sigil *Ohq* (Q) and the 2-6 Branch.

Important Star Forms: Vega, Aquila, Cygnus, Pleiades, Taurus, *Ursa* Major.

Magical Applications: Focusing and centring energy • Uniting diverse energies • Drawing power into the Mortal Realm • Invoking star power and Primal Utterance • Dispersal or release of spirits and energy.

Visionary Gateway: Light pours in dual streams from a horned moon, merging into one stream before you. You walk into the streak of silver moonlight and find yourself in a faery landscape. In turn, you meet a cow, a stag and a bird that lead you to a River that swirls with stars and spirals of earth memory...

Oracular Meanings: Focus • Flowing together • Union of opposites • Fusion of energies • Bridging realms • Fountaining energies • Sacred folly • Inspirations • Natural intuition • The centre, ever moving yet enduring • A goal • A dilemma • Two paths open, an instinctive choice, overcoming inhibition leads to freedom of choice • New life • Accepting two sides of an issue and realising a third stronger position.

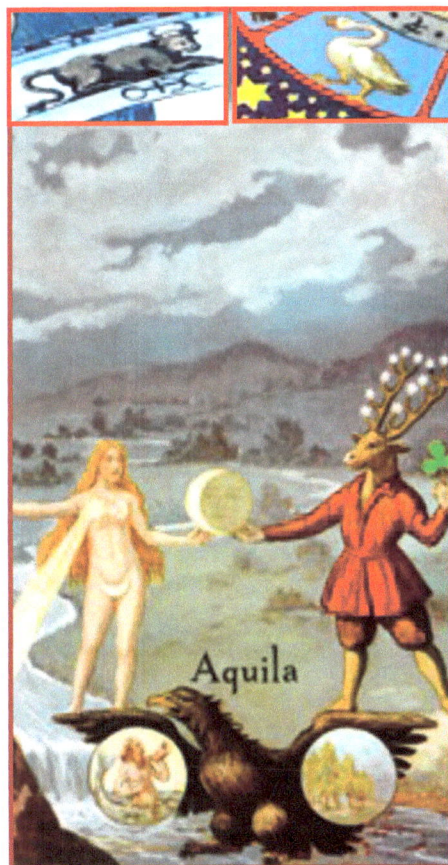

This detail from an alchemical Rosicrucian illustration shows some intriguing connections to the Faery Tradition. A Stag-headed man with star-studded antlers holds a shamrock in one hand while with his other hand he supports the moon with a Goddess standing in a stream. In the foreground is an Eagle.
Alchemical Rosicrucian illustration. 1698

Bo'ah (B Sigil):
The Wizard's House. The Hut

General Significance:
Bo'ah indicates lineage, including spiritual heritage, the thread or line of the ancestors, the Otherworld Teachers and Way-Showers. The sigil is itself suggestive of early meander signs. A Human landscape expressing Faery.

Bo'ah signifies what makes us feel whole (our spiritual "home" or tradition), where your heart is in terms of dedication to a specific spiritual path or "House of Illumination." On a universal level, this is the cosmic structure or harmonic pattern comprised of the balance and harmony of the Elements, the building blocks of the cosmos, our cosmic dwelling.

Thus **Bo'ah's** power is that of a sacred landscape or Temple. One's personal sacred space, the body, soul, the magical system as mediator of sacred presence and magical power. Blood lines and the magical properties of blood. Thus this Sigil relates to one's Way to wholeness, where faery, human, and Green fire are harmoniously expressed and embodied.

Base Position on the Faery Tree: Branch 6-8, Harmony and Illumination.

Important Star Forms: Sun, Mercury, Milky Way.

Magical Applications: Connecting with ancestral powers and presences • Awakening the Faery Covenant • Tuning human activity with Faery • Building bridges across time• Reconnecting the Covenant •Genetic Magic.

Visionary Gateway: You stand with your Co-walker before the mound of a portal Tomb. You follow your Reflex into the Mound and find yourself in a wondrous place...

Oracular Meanings: Matters resonating across time and place • The path to harmony, illumination Your way of wholeness • Regeneration of self through fusion with ancestral powers • A familial matter resolved • Harmony with nature • Gateway to wisdom • Initiation • Beginning of a road whose end is unknown • Entering a situation that appears convoluted like a labyrinth or maze.

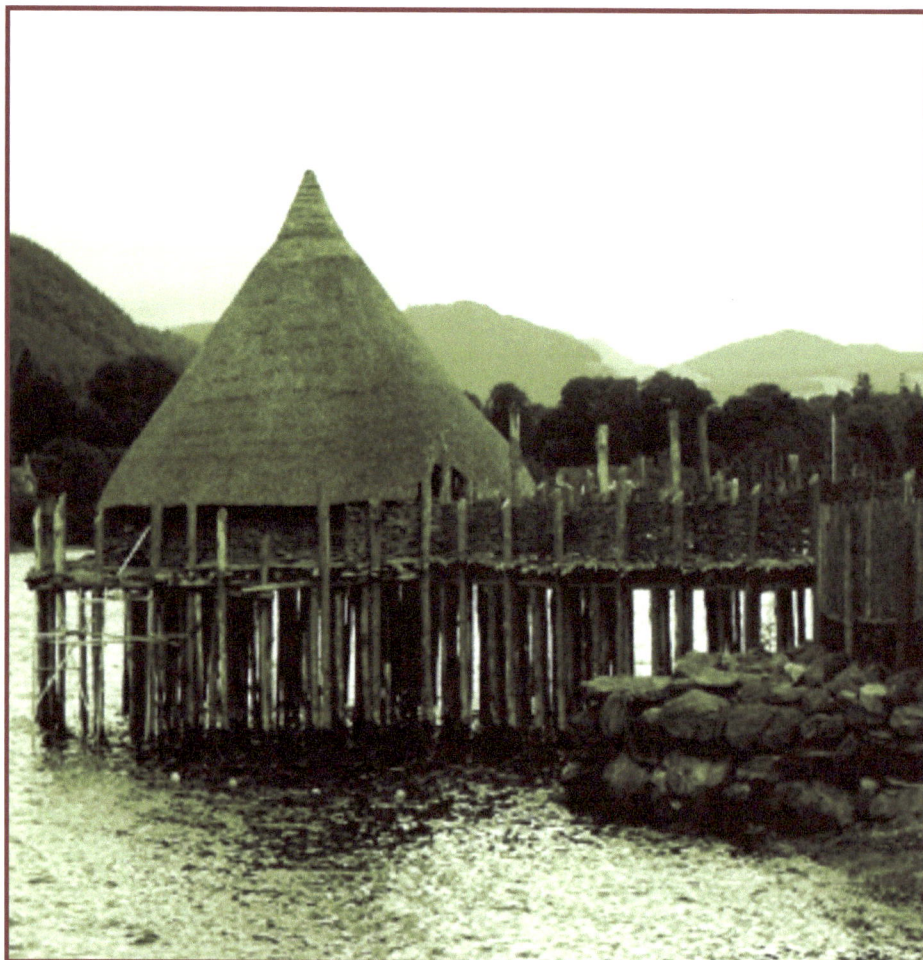

Many ancient peoples in Celtic countries lived in Crannog houses like the one pictured above, built about 5000 years ago in Loch Tay. Scotland

Cu (C sigil):
The Hedge.
The Enclosure

General Significance:
The sigil *Cu* (coo) reflects the great anabolic or building powers that transmute the primordial Elements into the forms of the physical world. *Cu* is the bountiful vision of the earth, the ingathering of abundance. *Cu* signifies the open-ended paradisal matrix, *Tír na nÓg*, the land of Faery, The regenerating vision and experience of nature. *Cu* enables physical reality as a means of illumination through transmuted or transfigured awareness and perception. The power of *Cu* transforms the vision of the initiate. Beatific, it infuses with love and art.

This is a protective power, as a mother bountiful and generous, fruitful and abundant. It is the womb of Earth, the Goddess whose body is earth and whose garment nature. Mother of the Faery Child who also births the faery landscape.

Base Position on the Faery Tree: Branch 4-7, fusing Peace, Compassion, Givingness, and Victory, Attainment, Attraction.

Important Star Forms: Luna, Venus, Evening Star, Dark Queen (Cassiopeia), Great Rift as womb of the Goddess in Milky Way.

Magical Applications: Drawing down the moon • Aligning issues or situations with lunar cycles • Setting a circle or magical enclosure.

Visionary Gateway: A crescent moon appears and becomes the arms of the goddess. She plays stellar rays like a harp, unearthly sounds fill the air, an image appears within her arms and descends to the ground before you…

Oracular Meanings: The blessings of a peaceful, rhythmic life • The place where you receive nurturing in your life, also love and generosity • Placing a situation or outcome in the arms of the Goddess • Lunar cycles affecting the outcome of a situation • Protecting and nurturing an idea or vision • Bringing something to birth.

Hedgerows were used in ancient times to define territory and contain livestock as well as for defensive purposes Above an ancient Cornish bank topped with gorse.

Do'ah (D sigil):
The Gate, GateKeeper.

General Significance:
Do'ah signifies the crossing of a threshold; The Guardian as mediator of initiatory wisdom. **Do'ah** has a deep connection to the power of attraction as a means of achieving wholeness or harmony. It is the power that opens and deepens experience.Triangles in various forms refer to womanhood and to Woman as the door of life and are abundant from early times. Engraved, triangular stones representing vulva have been found at the Chauvet cave complex (*circa* 30,000BCE). Triangles, apex up, also represent mountains, which in magical lore are places of access to transcendent realities. **Do'ah** signifies Faery doors, portals, passageways and channels. It is the power of ingress and egress, of entry and exit, transition from one state or experience to another. As the power that controls access, **Do'ah** represents guardianship of the entrance to the mysteries of the Faery Landscape, the UnderRealm, and the Stars. By extension this includes guardianship and mediation of initiatory wisdom. Has a deep connection to the power of attraction as a means of achieving wholeness or harmony. It is the power that opens and deepens experience.

Base Position on the Faery Tree: Branch 6-7, Harmony and Attainment or Beauty and Attraction.

Important Star Forms: Venus, Luna, Morning Star, Andromeda, Great Rift, as portal or lock on the river of stars. Faery Gates at Solstice points Pole Star.

Magical Applications: Opening and closing gates or locks • Guarding or warding a centre or the directions • Creating a Faery Door.

Visionary Gateway: A stone door appears in a hillside, a star shines in the dark. You go in and take the star out. It changes into an object that represents wisdom or knowledge that you require...

Oracular Meanings: The end and beginning of a quest • Attainment or initiation through Harmony and Beauty • A woman of power and influence • The way is open • Opportunities appearing • Wisdom gained from experience • Secrets revealed • Veils removed.

Portal Tombs such as the one rendered in this painting are both Shrines of the ancestors and gateways to the OtherWorld.P detail from The Mound, painting by coleston Brown 2007

Esh (E sigil):
The Faery Flag●
The Crow's Foot.

General Significance:
Esh signifies foresight, mental activity, clear sightedness; Clarity of Thought. One of the vowel sigils, Esh is mobile and moves with the Faery Fool. *Esh* represents new beginnings, dawn, rise of sun, moon and wandering stars. Spring. New Life. Song and word, Bird feet appear as early pictographs and petroglyphs throughout the world.

Direction: East

Element: Primal Air

Base Position on the Faery Tree: Branch 10-8. Same as *Ah*.

Important Star Forms: Gemini, Taurus, Pleiades, Cygnus, Aquila, Corvus, Milky Way.

Magical Applications: Setting a centre; Casting light ● Casting Oracles ● Mediating ritual energies ● Casting a Circle ● Opening an issue ● Severing the unessential ● Recitation.

Visionary Gateway: Follow bird tracks to a hollow tree with a hole in the trunk like a window. Look through and see future events or rising energies (possibly stars or situations)...

Oracular Meanings: Beginning a cycle ● New ideas ● Birth of an Enterprise or idea ● Rising or ascending energies ● Gradual illumination ● Life giving energy ● seeding energies ● Song, breath, and spoken expression ● Knowing which way the wind is blowing, Launch of a new Venture ● Awareness of tradition (Faery Flag) ●

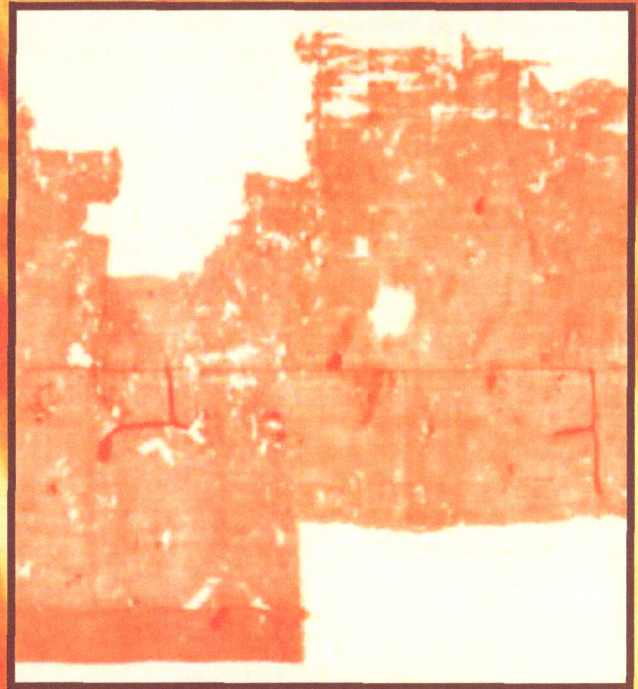

The famed Fairy Flag of Dunvegan, Scotland. Said to have been gifted by a Faery Woman, who having borne a child of one of the Chieftains of the Clan McCleod, wrapped the child in a blanket when she left. Shown here in backgound with the horn of Rob Mor.
Inset the remains of the Flag today.

Fir'eh (F sigil):
The Navigator, The Compass.

General Significance:
Fir'eh relates to the spiralling or circling force of regeneration. Serpentine figures, snakes, and double spirals similar to the *ƒ* form appear from 13,000 BC in the Megalithic cultures of Europe. **Fir'eh** denotes the spiralling, rising, the winding and unwinding power of the fire within or Faery serpent force. This is the power of regeneration, of spiritual force, vitality or strength. **Fir'eh** relates to creative energy in general and sexual energy in particular. In universal terms **Fir'eh** links to the axial life force of the cosmos, cycling or spiralling from one level to another. It can thus denote sublimation or degeneration of creative power.

Base Position on the Faery Tree: Branch 8-9, between the foundational energies and the illumined intellect or glory. Mental force, imagination, creative vision. Raising of the sexual energies and magical employment of regenerating power through control and containment within hermetic or formal ritual patterns.

The Centring Sigils

Several of the Sigils function as signs for setting a centre or consecrating a sacred space. in addition to the Vowel Sigils: A,E,I,O,U,; centring sigils include D,J,K,T,V,W,X,and Y. Technically, of course, any Sigil can be used to set a spiritual Centre, but these have a special application, depending on the purpose to which the sacred space is being consecrated.

Important Star Forms: Venus Mercury, Serpentis, Cygnus, Scorpio

Magical Applications: Moving power from one level to another • Navigating spirals of time and being • Bringing creative force across the realms.

Visionary Gateway: A Keeper of secrets appears with living sigil as key to unlock door of Faery Lock Keepers' house. Opens and leads you into a faery landscape...

Oracular Meanings: Navigating a situation • Unlocking secrets • Release from bondage or captivity • Releasing power • Sexual arousal • Creative inspiration • Turning events to one's advantage • Returning something to a prior state.

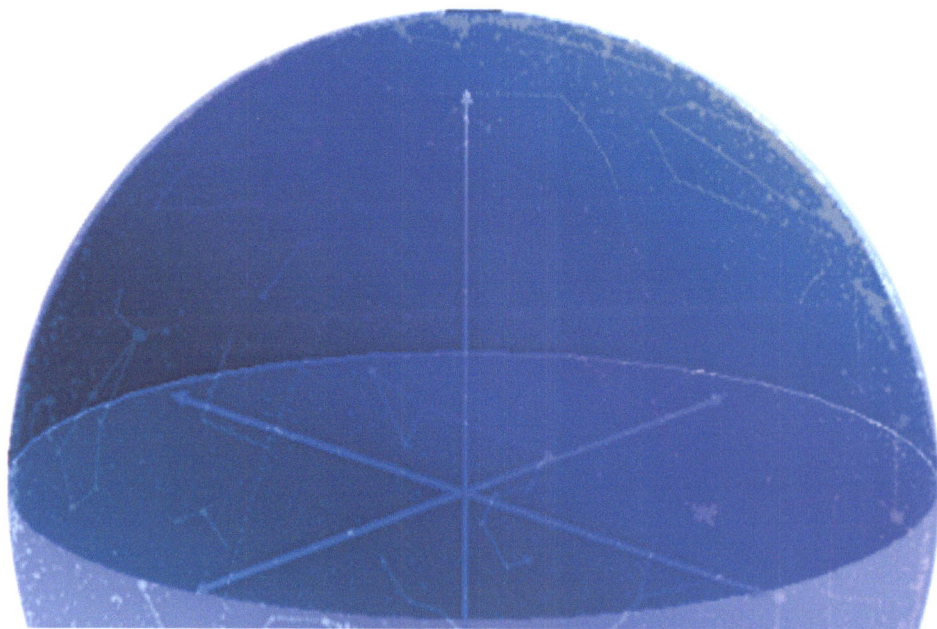

The Dome of Stars and the Sacred Directions.

Og (G sigil):
The Faery Boat, The Map.

General Significance:
Og signifies the vessel of vision as means of transportation between the Worlds. Moon emblems may simultaneously designate a magical hill and a wave. *Og* can denote the Moon Boat and Faery Ship

Og denotes the power to sustain or survive though seemingly difficult experiences. It is a means of transport, hence *Og* betokens spiritual vision (a meaning also indicated by the connection with the moon). The visionary power is the key to traversing the realms of the OtherWorld, especially in connection with initiatory experiences. Other expressions embodied in the power of *Og* are perseverance, memory and vitality (storage). Central too, to *Og* is the idea of preparation for the life-journey or incarnation-- this latter perhaps in the form of genetic predispositions or "spiritual gifts" that become active upon the quest for self-realisation. Thus the power of *Og* can be linked with the power of Grace as an active, enabling energy in the universe.

Base Position on the Faery Tree: Branch 9-10 fusing foundational, regenerative images or energies and the urge or impulse to completion. Insights into the deeps of Earth and being, and the underworld. Passing the (lesser) Guardians on the path of spiritual development or personal integration. One's preparedness for such adventure.

Important Star Forms : Luna, Saturn, Sun, Earth Star.

Magical Applications: Meeting the Guardian of the Threshold • Seeking Guidance • Making a magical map • Manifesting intentions or beings • Invoking inherent abilities that will be of help in a given situation.

Visionary Gateway: A silver ship appears out of a white mist. A Faery woman on board takes you on a journey to a sacred mound within the misty land, A gift is offered….

Oracular Meanings:
Dreams • Protection • Finding a way • Survival • Nourishment • Hidden opportunities revealed • Appropriately armed or enabled • Safe passage through a difficult situation • A journey or adventure • Grace • A gift • Hidden resources are discovered • Following intuition•Trust• Faith.

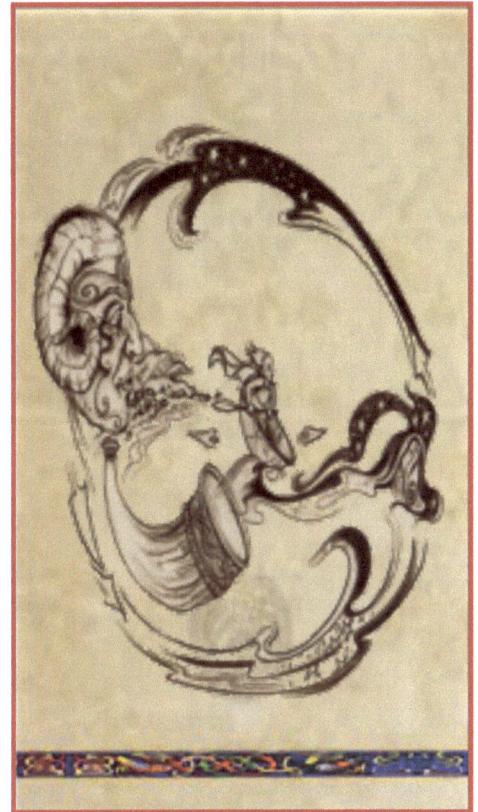

Above: The Haven Master and Faery Child by Jessie Skillen 2013; Below The Faery Ship Coleston Brown 2007

Hu (H sigil):
The Faery Glass, The Mirror. The Reflex.

General Significance:
Hu denotes the ability to see beyond walls or boundaries. It is the mirroring of earth and stars. Hu is Consciousness reflected in nature and its rhythms. This Sigil indicates transition, expansion, insight, farsight, seeing into the patterns of land and stars, having or being given the permission of the Goddess to merge with nature in its many forms and thence to look into the future or past.

Hu Signifies the transmission of creative energy through knowledge and compassion. **Hu** also betokens change and transformation by symbiosis, or reflection of being.

Base Position on the Faery Tree: Branch 2-4, Wisdom and Compassion/Harmony signifying beneficent influence, stellar or destinal power bringing Peace.

Important Star Forms: Jupiter, Venus, Luna (Uranus).

Magical Applications: Working with the Reflex ● Changing through relating to ancestral and Faery presences ● Bringing Clarity to specific situations ● Summoning allies ● Assembling support.

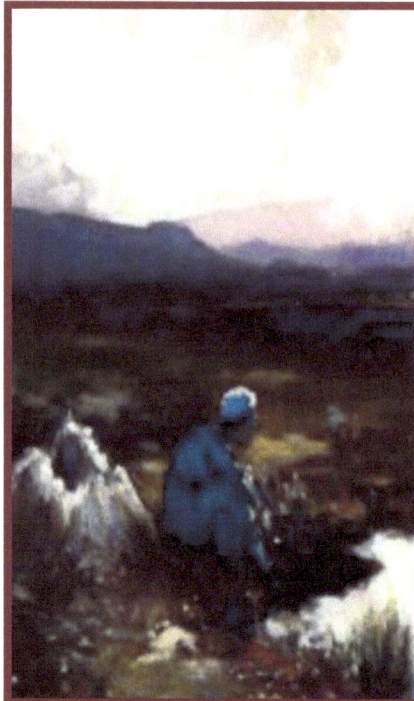

Figure 11: In this detail from The Watcher be A.E. (George Russel), the Reflex or Co-walker mirrors a woman gazing at her reflection in a stream.

"They call this Reflex-man a Co-walker, every way like the Man, as a Twin-brother and Companion, haunting him as his shadow... These Companions make themselves known and familiar to Men; other wise, being in a different State and Element, they neither can nor will easily converse with them."

~ **Robert Kirk,** *The Secret CommonWealth, 1691.*

Visionary Gateway: You stand on a bridge looking into the river flowing beneath. Currents and eddies swirl into the shape of Hu, and within the circles of that pattern a face appears. Your Co-walker/Reflex rises from the water— a being in synchronicity with you and your life. Within the water you see visions of how your actions effect faery and vice versa...

Oracular Meanings: Reflection ● Emulation ● A borrowed or stolen image ● Self image ● Role playing ● Mimicry ● Projecting self onto a situation envy ● Identifying with another person, situation or event ● Celestial patterns ● Compassionate action ● Empathy ● Magical dreams.

Reflection and reversal are key principles of faery contact. Bronze mirrors were likely used for skrying in ancient times, and would have been an effective way of conjuring the Co-walker. Above, a Romano-Celtic Mirror.

Ai (I Sigil):
The Faery Stick, TheWizard's Staff. The Spear.

General Significance:
Ai denotes creative power, passion, focus, fusing opposites. This Sigil signifies the Way of the Warrior, resolution through active force, Spiritual Will, Creative focus. *Ai* also resonates with Summer, as an expression of full solar energy. *Ai* signifies the centre of the Solar World, Pivot of the Life Cycle, Hidden stars. Control of the life Force. Signifies increase growth and centralised power in the Mortal World. One of the vowel sigils.

Direction: South

Element: Primal Fire

Base Position on the Faery Tree: Branch 10-8 Same as Ah.

Important starforms: Earth Star, Saturn, Mercury Mars. Aires Leo, Sagittarius, Saggita.

Magical Applications: Stilling energies • Focussing and channelling power • Uniting people, spirits or situations energetically • Opening a sacred space • Spiralling force running through seed centres of the Three Wheels and Realms • Command of the Elements.

Visionary Gateway:
In the GreenWood a Faery Wizard appears before you and strikes his walking stick thrice on a round Stone…

Oracular Meanings:
Peacemaking • Passion • Creative energy • Flow of power • Controlling self and others • Focus • Fighting for a cause • Opposites reconciled • Warmth • Open • Honest demeanour • Teaching inspired by faery • Support • Sustaining energies • Casting light • Guiding by starlight

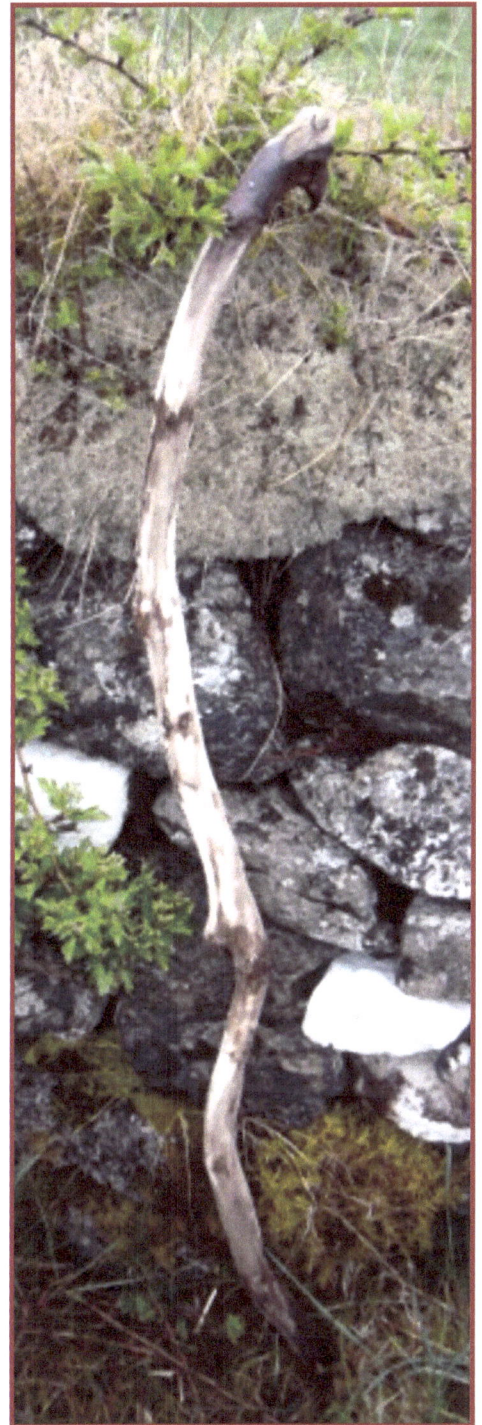

The teachings and traditions of Faery Sticks are stll known and practiced in Celtic lands. Above a Faery stick from County Sligo, Ireland.

Djee'ah (J sigil):
The Fetch,
The Arousal.

General Significance:
This Sigil denotes joy as a power in the universe. It also signifies the strike of the Faery serpent, The coiling and uncoiling of power around an axis, awakening or full functioning of power centres within the body and the Earth. *Djee'ah* betokens inward spiralling to the centre of creation, and outward spiralling as liberation from unending rotation or life-cycles.

Djee'ah's geometry of a spiral of energy and a terminating line suggests winding and unwinding power for a definite end or purpose. It is, of course, also suggestive of a hook.

As a development of the spiral of motion and energy often in terms of 4 worlds or Quadrants. *Djee'ah* often signifies an awakening facilitated by the Fetch or Faery Other. The Fetch is closely linked to the powers of attraction and repulsion, and to the feeling of falling in love that is a hallmark of Faery human relations. Problems sometimes occur when the Mortal and Faery energies are confused and people fall in love with faery Allies of other humans. On the other hand, if rightly understood and appreciated, the Fetch can be of great assistance in interpersonal relations.

Base Position on the Faery Tree: Branch 7-10, denotes a fusion of Attraction and the urge to completion expressed as, triumph or mastery over personal elemental energies (elemental Psyche) and cycles or incarnation. Also, the Quest and attainment/discovery of the Grail or Cosmic Centre.

Important Star Forms: Saturn, Earth Star, Venus. Mars, Mercury

Magical applications: Initiation energies • Casting glamours • Healing • Distance working • Polarity magic • Working with faery animals • Working with the fetch.

Visionary Gateway: You stand at the centre of an ancient stone labyrinth. A trilithon gate is before you. Your Faery Other appears at the gate and steps through to guide you out of the Labyrinth and into a wondrous light-filled land...

Oracular Meanings: New beginnings • Initiation • Falling in love •becoming enamoured, or enchanted •infatuation • Healing • Happiness • Influence of a lover. • Positive encounters with animals.

The Fetch or Faery Other is one of the type of being known as the Faery Companions, which also includes the Reflex and the Faery Animal. The Animal and the Fetch are closely inked in Faery Seership, the one often morphing in into the other. Painting by AE (George Russel)

Aeikuo (K sigil):
The Hand,
The Faery Child,
The Covenant.

General Significance:
Aeikuo, signifies contact, containment, openness and sincerity. It denotes the hand as the instrument of building, making, creating, counting, measuring, harmlessness & peacemaking. Also the framework that bestows or gives harmony. Thus Aeikou also refers to symbol systems, containers of creation, etc. As a sign of two hands outstretched in opposite directions, this sigil signifies the renewed Human-Faery covenant. At the centre of the renewed covenant is the Faery Child, whose very name *Aeikou* (pron. Ay-koo), indicates one who lives in the midst of opposites (i.e. the Four Elements.) The Child fuses opposites and is neither male nor female but an androgynous presence that carries and contains our individual Co-walker and Fetch (Faery Other).

Base Position on the Faery Tree: Branch 6-4, linking harmony and compassion. Signifies the balance and peace or poise, fulfilment and givingness, compassion or generosity.

Important Star Forms: The Milky Way, Auriga, Orion, The Sun, Luna, Five ancient wandering Stars.

Magical applications: Opening the Path to Faery • General Ritual Opening • Magical Gate Opening • Sealing an agreement • Activation of Giving and Taking Powers • Form as a vehicle for spiritual force or expression of archetypes.

Visionary Gateway: You Meet the Faery Queen at a holy well and join hands beneath the water. The sigils become active and flow from her to you... (see above Vision of Etain, page 5.)

Oracular Meanings: Finding a balance • Handling opposing influences • Offering friendship • Giving and taking • Expressing polarities • Building something.

Background from a Painting by AE (George Russell):The Faery Child, which appears in Magical vision as an androgynous Youth, is intimately linked to the souls of the Priests and Priestesses of the Faery Covenant who mediate it and thus has for them a certain psychological dynamic,connected to the archetype of the Self; Right Above: The Hand is an ancient image,known from Palaeolithic times, linking the Human to Presences in the Land; Right Below:the Faery Band of Friendship. Acrylic on wood by Jessie Skillen 2010.

Eil (L sigil):
The Shepherdess, The Crafter.

General Significance: Eil denotes the driving power of Sacred Presence. Bardic energy, inspiration, The play of life experience positive and negative as a means of spiritual development or evolution. That which motivates us, spurs us on, yet simultaneously causes us to avoid certain types of experience, situation, thought or occurrence. Presence of Faery. **Eil** is the energy or inspiration of the craftsperson, whether smith or poet.

Base Position on the Faery Tree: Branch 4-5 fusing Giving and Taking, signifies life lessons, even karmic connections to the past. The resolution or rectification of that which is hindering progress, whether in the nature of inhibitions or excesses.

Important Star Forms Jupiter, Mars, Sun.

Magical applications: Initiating a flow of energy or series of events • Commanding Presences, and Powers • Calling on the Goddess • Summoning the Concourse • Healing and protection.

Visionary Gateway: You are bending over a stream to drink. An ancient woman, her hands and face blackened by soot, arches over a crooked walking stick as she shuffles past. The faint sound of a forge comes clearer as you follow her. Sparks fill her footprints. She enters a small stone hut through a low linteled doorway. After a brief while you follow. You swing open the door and part the leather hanging. A great golden light engulfs you.....

Oracular Meanings: A gift given and a gift received • Exchange • Motivation • Inspiration in art and craft • The guiding power of destiny or divine force • Avoiding hurtful experience • Riding a wave of energy or influence to success • Control and guidance.

The Goddess Brigid appears in Celtic Lore as shepherdess of bees and animals. She is also a blacksmith, a crafter, and a poet. Above, Brigid painting by Jessie Skillen, 1998 Inset: Weyland's smithy, From the Ardre Image Stone

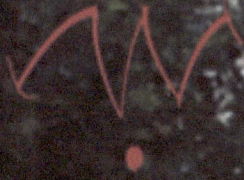

Mu (M sigil):
The Cascade ,
The Faery Horse.

General Significance:

The "M sign" and its association with water or, more abstractly, with flow, is widely dispersed through time and place. It appears among the earliest cave signs, yet retains its essential shape and meaning to the present day: the idea of flow, emotions, reflection, cleansing and purifying. *Mu* signifies undulation or oscillation of energy, movement within the ocean of being. It denotes primal, undifferentiated Being, sacrifice through merging, emerging from the prima material or stuff of creation, the reversal that is inherent in reflection, rising and falling energies, a cascade of power, being in the Stream.

Base Position on the Faery Tree: Branch 3-6 fusing Enfoldment and Harmony, the universal matrix or Great Mother and the hidden pattern or spiritual structure of Matter.

Important Star Forms: Saturn, Sun, Luna, Cancer. Beehive, Milky Way (Uranus, Neptune).

Magical Applications: opening a sacred space to flows of energy • Summoning the torrent of Powers and presences that flow in streams that whirl and turn within the womb of inner earth • Sending out fluctuating, rising and falling energy streams timed tidally or tuned to stellar cycles.

Visionary Gateway: You are on a narrow stone bridge that ends in a wall of water. A cascade falls before you ending in foamy swirls below in a pool of blue and green. A white horse appears behind you on the bridge and offers to take you through the cascade. You mount the horse's back and ride through ....

Oracular Meanings: Passing a barrier • Overwhelmed by feeling • A cleansing purifying experience • Succour • Unexpected help arrives • Faery assistance is given.

Background photo:Dargle horsetail waterfall, Ireland 2003; Inset Morigu, the faery Mare. 2013

Nu (N Sigil)
The Serpent Strike,
The Faery Cord
(sidhe corda beag).

General Significance:
Nu denotes the ability to move with the universal flow of energy and to tap it for regeneration. Thus it is linked to spiritual transformation, death, and rebirth. *Nu* embodies the power of the Faery Serpent and the Salmon of wisdom. Fishes and serpents are common in Palaeolithic cave art and signify the ability to move with the universal flow of energy and to tap it for regeneration. *Nu* is one of the "Z" sigils or signs of illumination, signifying awakening. It is connected to the *Imbas forosnai,* which is a form of clairvoyance or illumination known from early Irish texts and tales, as, for instance, in the story of Fionn and the Salmon of Wisdom.

The association of the fish with the womb of the goddess occurs since Palaeolithic times and reinforces the meanings of birth, death, rebirth. Hence the consonance of the womb and tomb in archaic magical forms.

Base Position on the Faery Tree: Branch 3-5 fusing Understanding and Power of Taking; Enfoldment through the catabolic power. Initiatory death, which returns one to the Great Mother or universal matrix where rebirth becomes possible.

Important Star Forms: Saturn, Mars, Pisces, Scorpio (Uranus)

Magical applications: Raising inner power • The serpent strike • Cord casting • Invoking inspiration • Calling on regenerative powers • Evoking energetic movement.

Visionary Gateway: You kneel at the edge of a holy well. A Salmon swims up from the bottom. The fish transforms into a serpent. There is a rowanberry in its mouth ….

Oracular Meanings: A situation regenerated • Eureka moment • Sudden awakening • Feeling reborn • Inspired and alive • In some circumstances can signify lies and deceit.

In Scotland, Brigid is known as Bride, and is associated the Brown Adder and the beginning of Spring (Imbolc)

*"On the day of Bride,
the serpent will come forth from the mound,*

*I will not molest the serpent,
And the serpent shall not molest me"*

Carmina Goedelica 1900

Brigid's associations with the fires of inspiration link her to both Rowan Trees and Serpents.

O'ah (O Sigil):
The Treasure,
The River,
Faery Gold,
TheFaery Cord
(sidhe corda mor).

General Significance:
O'ah bridges into *Ah* ~ the two are magically resonant on different levels. Ah generates, *O'ah* completes and enfolds. This Sigil signifies physical sensation, completion, wholeness, fulfilment, the heart's desire, peace, deep wisdom, that which fulfils; stability, equanimity, and earthiness. *O'ah* denotes the Green Awareness, bounty, structure, patterns, security, growth, expansion.

Direction: North

Element: Primal Earth

Base Position on the Faery Tree:
Branch 10-8 Same as Ah .

Important Star Forms: Earth Star, Saturn, Jupiter, Sun, Mercury, Milky Way (Pluto)

Magical applications: Opening a Path • Calling upon Tradition • Invoking acceptance • Opening and Closing • Treading the Circle • Censing or scenting a sacred space • Pledges and Oaths.

Visionary Gateway: You are walking through a lush green wood. You spy a green cord or vine coiled on the ground and pick it up. As you pull on it you realise it is attached to a ring in a copper door in a great Yew Tree. you swing the door open and see a spiral stair of tree roots descending into the earth .....

Oracular Meanings: Finding fulfilment • Contentment • Opportunity appears • Worthiness • Open-heartedness • Satisfaction • Finding a resource • A gift from faery • Equability • Generous spirit • Options are presented.

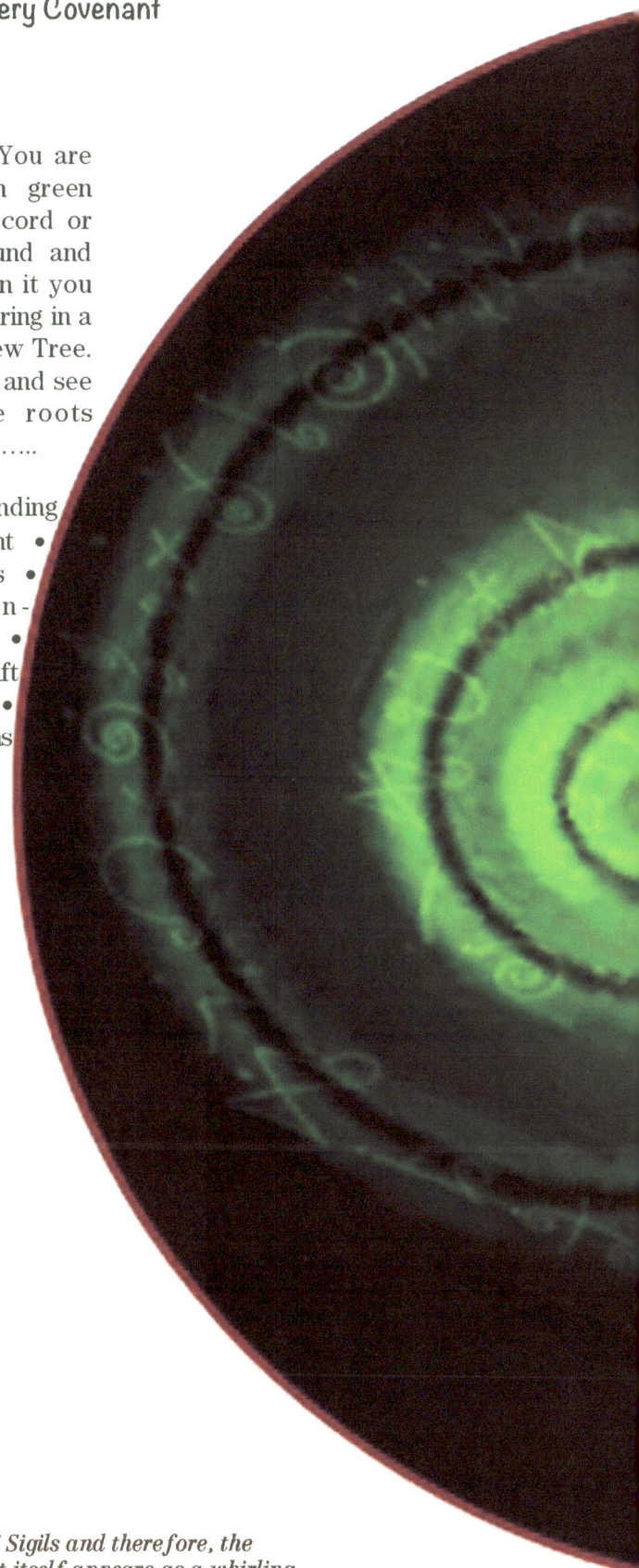

The Stream of Sigils and therefore, the Faery Covenant itself appears as a whirling Light within the UnderRealm. Above, The Stream of Sigils by Coleston Brown 2013

Phai (P Sigil):
The Utterer,
The Green Tongue.

General significance:

Phai denotes the mouth, as the vocal instrument emitting sounds of expression in the higher forms of song and speech and is thus a harmonising power. The mouth is also the instrument of ingestion, which catabolises, breaks down for digestion and so Phai is also an awakening, breaking power; This Even applies to listening and learning by breaking a subject down into manageable units; Teaching through oral tradition; Power of the Word or *Ur-Speech*, the Language of Angels or Faery, The secret Language of Birds, lost through mythic events such as the Tower of Babel or the rape of Faery Maidens. **Phai** betokens a Loss of connection with the Sacred through divisiveness, parochialism, provincialism, or through discursive thought/speech. This Sigil also signifies the Magic of building, construction or destruction through songs **or words of power.**

The Utterer may appear as male or female and in most mythologies is male. In the Faery Tradition this figure tends to be female, however. This is the presence that breaths forth the Stars and utters into being all shapes, colours and sounds. Soft sculpture by Jessie Skillen.

Base Position on the Faery Tree: Branch 6-5 fuses Harmony and Taking Power. The harmonic essence released by catabolic energy or breakdown.

Important Star Forms: Sun, Mars, Venus, Jupiter (Uranus).

Magical applications: Chant And Recitation • Invocation and Evocation • Charms • Runes • Blessings • Incantations • Elemental Calls and Faery Chants • Prophetic Utterance.

Visionary Gateway: You are in the Green wood. Singing birds alight in the trees, as bees hum all around. You listen carefully to their secret language…

Oracular Meanings: Charmed by word or song • Taking one into confidence • A confident • The words of a holy man or woman • Prophecy • Belief based on the charms of another • In certain circumstances can signify gossip or slander.

Ohq (Q Sigil):
The Faery Wheel,
The Exemplar.

General significance:
Ohq includes the act of following a spiritual paradigm or a mirroring of initiation through imitation or reenactment of sacred patterns. This Sigil may embody the power of regeneration through contact with immortals; resolution into stellar seeds or energy patterns; cycles or spirals of energy, time and space such as the life cycle, the seasons, "Great Years" or Major Spirals of Time. **Ohq** also betokens Faery time

Ohq is linked in particular to the cycles or circuits of the sun, moon and stars. The workings of Faery are temporally different to those of the Mortal World. Thus often Spiritual work with Faery will seem to occur in accelerated and condensed or slow-moving and relaxed time (see sidebar).

Base Position on the Faery Tree: Branch 2-6 Wisdom and

Harmony, seed power and cosmic structure or harmonic expression. Awareness through balance. Wisdom through Music, beauty, harmony of the spheres, (zodiacal tones) Conceptualisation of archetypal force, especially in terms of polar relationships.

Important Star Forms: Milky Way, Zodiac, Sun, Luna.

Magical Applications: Turning the Wheel or "spiral of time" • working in Faery time • Ritual or visionary cycles • Ritual Time.

Visionary Gateway: A man in an ill-fitting brown tunic is rolling an eight-spoked wheel in front of him. He stops suddenly, letting the wheel fall. It becomes a well. The Man beckons you to look in. Within you see the turning of day and night, the seasons and the whirling stars….

Oracular Meanings: Matters can seem delayed but are proceeding according to an inner time frame • Preoccupation with time • Impatience • Exigence or, alternately, Melancholy.

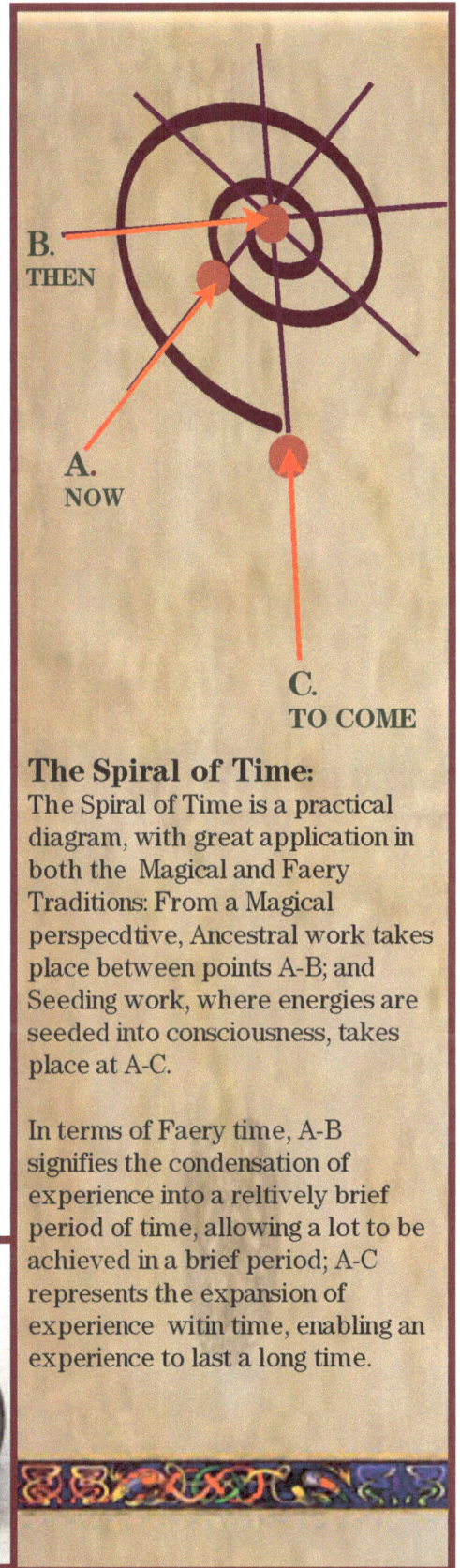

B. THEN

A. NOW

C. TO COME

The Spiral of Time:
The Spiral of Time is a practical diagram, with great application in both the Magical and Faery Traditions: From a Magical perspecdtive, Ancestral work takes place between points A-B; and Seeding work, where energies are seeded into consciousness, takes place at A-C.

In terms of Faery time, A-B signifies the condensation of experience into a reltively brief period of time, allowing a lot to be achieved in a brief period; A-C represents the expansion of experience witin time, enabling an experience to last a long time.

Rai (R Sigil):
The Youth,
The Fire in the Head.

General significance:
Rai indicates youthfulness, rejuvenation, innocence, immaturity, freshness beauty, clarity, fiery incandescent love. **Rai** may signify Presence of faery. Illumination. Sacred life-giving power. Rai also embodies and expresses spiritual radiance as the dissemination of inner wisdom or harmony.

Neolithic vases have been found with line figures inscribed on them with solar heads. These solar heads signify leadership, sovereignty, centrality. In ancient times the heads of holy persons were seen to radiate like, like a sun. Thus **Rai's** connection to the notions of illumination, sacred life-giving power, radiance or dissemination of inner wisdom or harmonious patterns. Rai also denotes perfection or original form (the head as a sphere or circle of birth and rebirth or eternal youth).

Base Position on the Faery Tree: Branch 9-6. Fusion of foundational energies and harmony (moon and sun). Reflection of beauty. Visions, psychic and spiritual. Edenic visions of foundation and harmony.

Important Star Forms: Luna, Sun, Personal Star of Destiny.

Magical applications: Renewing energies • Initiation • Invoking the faery child • Illuminating self through magical workings.

Visionary Gateway: A youth of indeterminate sex, with hair of flame, appears bearing a small twig. The youth lights the twig from the flames and plants it in the rich, dark earth where it grows into a mighty tree ...

Oracular Meanings: Rejuvenation or renewal of a person or situation • Innocence • Foolish or naive behaviour • Zest for life • Taking fresh look at something • A new perspective • A situation awaiting growth and maturation • Change in motivation.

Aegus Og. Faery expressionist painting by Coleston Brown

Shay (S Sigil):
The Weaving.
The Communion of Spirits,
The Judge.

General significance: Shay signifies weaving of patterns in harmony and evokes the image of weaving flames. In Palaeolithic signatory **Shay** is related to the double chevron and the "Z" sign. Its undulating shape links it to the serpent, in this case the serpent fire or spiritual flame.

Shay denotes a double flame or sun, spiritual, psychic, cosmic or physical. It thus signifies the Communion of Sprits, which comprises three interwoven streams: *The Primal Stream,*which is one's contact with Primal Presences and Powers; *The Stream Of Affinity,* which is one's initiatic Stream; and *The Convocation Of Ancestors.* **Shay** also signifies thesis, antithesis, synthesis as a magical process, and as a process of determination or judgment. In cosmic terms the process refers to force and form in a cosmic dance which yields a third force, of deep "plutonic" transformation. In negative aspect this is nuclear fission by artificial means. In

positive, the very process of creation. The double spiral suggests weaving motions and also the movement of Bees, both of which are important expressions of Faery.

Base Position on the Faery Tree: Branch 2-3, fusing enfoldment and wisdom and signifying decision or judgment. The weighing of polarities or concepts to arrive at a balance.

> Hush, dear, hush, I hear the wild bees humming
> Far away in the underworld where true love shall not part!
> ...William Sharp ~An Old Tale of Three.

Important Star Forms: Milky Way, Zodiac, Saturn, jupiter, Pole Star, Void, Earth Star (Pluto, Uranus).

Magical applications: Weaving Magic • Bee Magic • Working in The Communion of Spirits • magically resolving opposites, balancing elements and powers • Deep chthonic working with the Earth Star • Threading the Labyrinth.

Visionary Gateway: You are in the GreenWood. Bees fly from a hole at the roots of a Rowan tree. You see a light shining in the place the bees flew from...

Oracular Meanings: Judgement • discernment • seeing different sides to an argument or situation • Seeking Spiritual Advice • Seeking advice from Spirits • Weaving a solution to a problem.

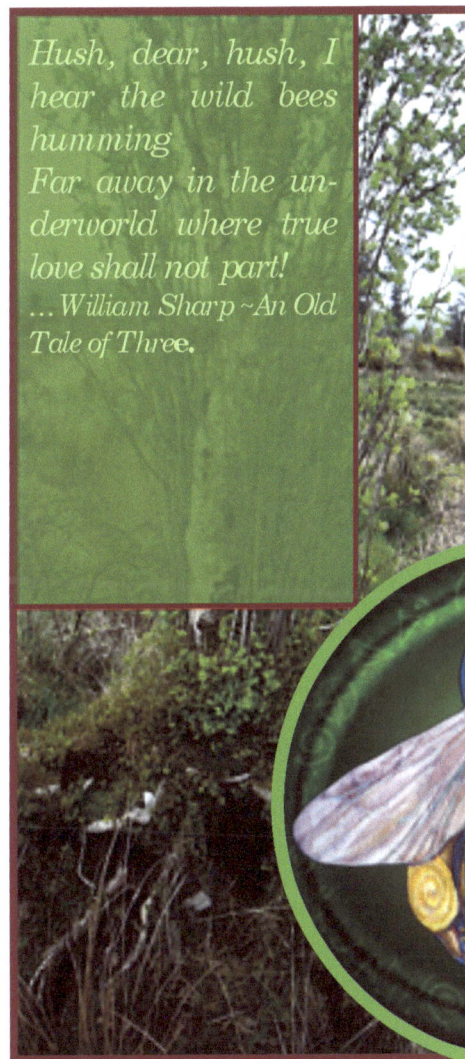

Bee on wood by Jessie Skillen &Rowan Tree, County Sligo, Ireland.

Ti (T sigil):
The Star,
The Sign.

General significance:
Ti betokens the source of being, the fourfold elemental way to and from the spiritual centre. Thus it signifies ones unique destiny or star; the confluence or influence of stellar powers, the Source; radiating light or clarifying vision.; cyclic temporal rotations or circuits.

Ti denotes a mark or cross as in a signature, one's own personal mark of destiny or one's star signature. X or + in ancient times was used to mark out by defining or focusing a centre, an area or object as particularly sacred. Possibly this was an early sign sign for a star.

In one sense, *Ti* signifies the original vision or primordial revelation of sacred space.

Base Position on the Faery Tree: Branch 1-6, Originating light fused with harmonic patterns. Hence the Spirit or source of being expressed as Self or "Higher" Self.

Important Star Forms: Pole Star, Sun, Luna, Earth Star.

Magical applications: Setting a centre • Creating a focus for worship or inspiration • Invoking destiny • Working with the cardinal directions • Circulating magical power in a temple or ritual • Threshold magic.

Visionary Gateway: You are on the edge of a bog, standing beneath an ancient tree, A white horn hangs from a branch…

Oracular Meanings: A sign is given • A happy place • Transformation of circumstances • A change of life • Fated • Fulfilling one's destiny.

The Star, painting by Coleston Brown 2008.

U'ah (U Sigil)
The Cauldron,
The Cave,
The Lake of Wonder.

General significance:

U'ah signifies the Caldron, the vessel and the cave, tomb and womb. It thus denotes emotion as a vehicle for spiritual force or the expression of archetypes. *U'ah* is that which carries, contains or contours. Imaged as a hollow, the cupped hand. Also the receptiveness or framework that bestows or gives harmony. As a Magical Form, the Cauldron is related to the whirlpool, which in Faery Tradition is linked to the confluence of the waters and the rising of inspiration from the Deep. From the Salmon of Wisdom, to Mananan of the Sea, the great water beings are widely sought and recognised as important contacts in the Faery Tradition.

Cauldron shaped bowls of land, such as those associated with the celtic tribe of the *Dubonni* near Gloucester, and Glastonbury*, seem to have played a part in ancient Celtic relations with the Land and Faery.

Direction: West

Element: Primal Water

Base Position on the Faery Tree: Branch 10-8 Same as *Ah*.

Important Star Forms: Earth Star, Mercury, Saturn, Jupiter Sun, Milky Way (Pluto, Neptune).

Magical applications: Creating a magical container • Sealing or consecrating a magical object • Drawing together a confluence of energies • Working with the Cauldrons of Poesy • Working from the depths.

Visionary Gateway: You are on the shores of a magical lake. The water swirls and drains revealing three ancient stone walls that meet at the centre of the lake. you walk along one of these walls until you see to a stone near the meeting point of the walls. There is a hole in his stone which drank the lake-water. You look into the hole and see a faint green mist rising below…

Oracular Meanings: Stirring emotions • Deep feelings • Turbulent times • Swept away • Overcome by circumstances • Calling on one's reserve • Nourishment • Bounty • Reward • Caring for or being cared for • Healing power • Inspiration and excitement • Transformation through art or music.

Gundestrop Cauldron., Denmark. 150-0 BC

---

* The latter is associated with the area of what is now popularly known as "The Glastonbury Zodiac." See my *Secrets of a Faery Landscape* for further indications and references.

Vo (V Sigil)
The Stone,
The Holestone,
The Hagstone,
GawkStone

General Significance:
Vo has to do with a centre or pole, a focus, which suggests a spiritual point or centralising power, the fusing of opposites into a central point of reflection and verity. *Vo* betokens originating light and stellar wisdom. The source embodied by the stars.

The V or chevron sign in Palaeolithic art probably represents the face (frontal) or horns of an animal such as a stag, goat or bull, or alternatively the beak of a bird (*see also* the Sigil *Ah*). *Vo* has some link also to the *Yai* sigil as the spinning distaff that appears in Palaeolithic art in connection with clusters of stars.

In practical terms, *Vo* denotes the spiritual leader or grand master/lady of a particular path. *Vo* signifies a boundary marker or stone. *Vo* is related to the Hole Stones that allow interchange and vision between the Worlds. *Vo* also links to hagstones that are used to look into Faery or otherwise employ the *Second Sight*.

The Turning of the
Stone

Come who know,
Come who will,
Come who dare,

Into the Silent Turning,
Into the Hollow Stone,
Into the Dark Unlearn-
ing,
Of body, blood and bone.

Out of the endless cir-
cles,
Into the Spiral grow,
Into the Silent Turning,
Into the Hallowed Flow,

Come who will,
Come who dare,
Come who know.

© 2004 Coleston Brown

Base Position on the Faery Tree: Branch 1-2 Source/Summit and Wisdom. Originating Light and stellar wisdom. The source embodied by the stars. Connecting with the source or facet of the jewel of truth for one's own spiritual destiny.

Important Star Forms: Pole Star. Milky Way, Zodiac (Uranus, Mars, Neptune, Pluto..

Magical applications: Seership • Scrying • Contacting spirits • Seeing energy patterns • Setting a Centre • Star Magic.

Visionary Gateway: You follow a stag up a hill and come opon a standing Faery stone. There is a hole in the stone, which you look through to view the Land...

Oracular Meanings: A new perspective • Taking a spiritual view of things • Taking a hit • Retribution • Collaboration • Joint venture • Focussing on the essentials.

left lower:The Hole Stone, Co Antrim, Northern Ireland, 1994.

left upper : A hagstone from Co Antrim, Northern Ireland.

Owth (W Sigil):
The Mound,
The Hill,
The Awakener.

General Significance:

Owth betokens high places, centres of the world or of matter, yet also the threshold of the Transcendent. High places where vision or overview is extended, the vantage point, sentinel power. Ambition or aspiration, centre of matter. Materialism or contact with the matrix. Might also represent trees or forest, thus the centre of nature. *Owth* is one of the "Z" signs.

In Palaeolithic times this sign merges with M sign (one of the z signs NMWRZS), though in reverse, meaning mountain peaks or hills rather than cascades of water. *Owth* is connected to the ancient Phoenician consonant *Ayin*, the eye, signifying the power of surveying or standing sentinel.*

---

* *Ayin* is in fact related to the development of the vowel O.

W is a form of the greek ω, omega.

Base Position on the Faery Tree: Branch 3-5, fusing the Enfolding and Taking Powers. Denotes awakening though both hard and beautiful experiences; the lightning flash; rude awakening. UnderRealm force, the reflection or restriction of reality in the UnderRealm. The power behind form and the form behind power.

Important Star Forms: Saturn, Mars, LunaEarth Star, Milky Way, Sagitta.

Magical applications: Sidhe magic • Sacred Tree Workings • Initiatory experience of passing the Guardian on the Threshold • Work with the spirits of the wood • The Faun • The Awakener of the Forest.

Visionary Gateway: You are following the flight of a green woodpecker when it alights on the portal stone of a faery Mound . A golden arrow is stuck in the earth before the mound. You pull the arrow out and the land bleeds. A Presence stirs within the Mound….

Oracular Meanings: Awakening • Shock • Fright • A positive surprise • Guarding • Protecting • Being stirred to life • Revivified and stimulated • Shadow projections • Illusions • Disillusionment.

But what of the Forest-Awakener? Who is he…., he is a moon-worshipper, the chorister of the stars, the incense-swinger before the altars of the dawn and though he is a child of the woods, he loves the thickets also."

William Sharp. ~ The Awakener

The Mound, painting by Coleston Brown © 2007

Xai (X Sigil)
The Tree,
The CrossRoads.

General Significance:
Xai is one of the "Z" signs. It is an upholding, balancing power. *Xai* denotes the Universal Tree, the lightning bolt flashing down to define the world axis as Tree. It is that which upholds, supports and maintains balance. *Xai* has a connection or attunement to various realms or inner aspects of Nature, linked with outer aspects. It signifies walking between the realms, and is thus connected the the magical form of the CrossRoads..

This Sigil gets its meanings from a confluence of significances for the X sign, known since Palaeolithic times, and an early pictograph representing a tent-pole or a staff, both of which latter, in archaic symbolism, signify the axis or vertical channel linking Land, UnderRealm and Stars.

It expresses and embodies *Xai* signifies the Wheel of the Moon in general. But also embodies an ancient sign for a star. Xai signifies balance between opposites or a point of rest. Hence its meaning of a crossroads, which have always favoured for the location of Inns and rest-stops.

Base Position on the Faery Tree: Branch 7-8, fusing Victory/attainment and glory/honour. The emotive and intellectual powers conjoined. Thus mental acuity tempered by emotional valuation and vice versa.

Important Star Forms: Venus, Mercury, Sun, Earth Star, Luna.

Magical applications: Setting a centre • The Quarters • Crossroads Magic • Magic of Reconciliation and redemption • Connection to Self through Fetch, Reflex, or Holy Guardian Angel.

Visionary Gateway: You are standing under a Tree at a crossroads. An animal appears beside you and leads you down one of the Roads....

Oracular Meanings: Reaching a crossroads • Choice • A decision must be made • Matters to be weighed • Seeking a balanced solution • Taking a new path • Rest and respite.

Figure 25: An Altai/Scythian gold artifact, showing a Tree Mother at a Crossroads, A traveller rests his head in her lap. The woman's headdress mirrors that found in the tomb of the famed Altai Ice Maiden.

Yai (Y Sigil),
The Seed,
The Fist,
The Distaff

General Significance: Yai denotes a "centre" or concentration of sacred energy. Thus **Yai** is one of several Centring Sigils, **Yai** also signifies a creative spark or seed; a point of the weaving or spreading of creation; a Faery Knot expressing and embodying the spark of being, the essential self. **Yai** betokens creative action or potential.

Yai is connected to ancient marks signifying the closed-hand or fist. Related early pictographs suggest a whirling cross. As a basic shape reflected in Palaeolithic art **Yai** signifies a sprouting seed or axial pole and later a distaff. (*see also* Vo and Xai).

Base Position on the Faery Tree: Branch 1-3. Fusing the Source and the Enveloping power, this branch denotes Knowledge that the Source or Seed contains the pattern or destiny of the Tree. Thus the meaning of awareness of potential, understanding of archetypes or matrices of creation.

Important Star Forms: The Pole Star, Earth Star, Saturn,

Magical applications: Seed magic • Setting a centre • Invoking power • Mediating • Flowing energy round a circle • Seeding images into consciousness.

Visionary Gateway: You meet a woman with hair of flowers. Bees hum around her. She holds a distaff to which is attached a many coloured thread that she follows into a Labyrinth. You accompany her into the heart of the maze … and out again …

Oracular Meanings: A sign is given • A happy place • Planting a seed • Transformation of circumstances • A change of life • Fated • Fulfilling one's destiny • Setting something in motion.

"*A seer had told him of Orchil, the dim goddess who is under the brown earth, in a vast cavern, where she weaves at two looms. With one hand she weaves life upward through the grass; with the other she weaves death down- ward through the mould; and the sound of the weaving is Eternity, and the name of it in the green world is Time., through all, Orchil weaves the weft of Eternal Beauty, that passeth not, though its soul is Change. Not cruel, relentless, impotently, anarchic, chaotically po- tent, this Mater Genetrix. We see her thus, who are flying threads in the loom she weaves.*"

William Sharp ~ At The Turn of the Year.

Inset upper: an unusual leaf-shaped maze from Dorset;
Inset lower: Frigg Weaving.

Zah (Z Sigil)
Thunderbolt, Sword

General Significance:
Zah denotes awakening, immediate and dramatic as if lightning struck. It also represents a delineation of opposites or polarities, linking the four points of the compass (directions) in specific magical fashion. The concepts of polarity and descending or ascending force suggest the sexual power or serpent force.

Zah links to both the Phoenician letter *Zayin*, meaning weapon or sword, and an ancient pictograph likely representing lightning, the sword of the thunder god. As a Palaeolithic sign it appears as early as 30,000 BC on a reindeer bone possibly as a resurrection or initiatic sign.

Base Position on the Faery Tree: Branch 9-7 The sustaining, weaving Power fused with the power of enchantment or attraction supports and emphasises the meanings of polarity and sexuality mentioned above.

Important Star Forms: Luna Venus, mars, (Uranus)

Magical applications: Weather magic • Calling down the fire • Initiation • Rites of awakening and illumination.

Visionary Gateway: A flash of lightning over a dark landscape illuminates a Path across the bog ...

Oracular Meanings: Being shown a way • Revelation • Clarifying matters • Shock • Awakening • Inspiration • Unexpected events • Sudden windfall • Sexual awakening • Deception • Being conned • Brazen advantage • Attack.

Thorn (' Breath Sigil) Pause, Void

General Significance:

Not really a Sigil, but more of a placeholder, Thorn signifies Pause, rest, breath, respite, peacefulness, darkness, emptiness, sharp sorrow, longing.

Oracular Meanings:

Taking a break, resting, pausing. being stopped, hitting a snag; finding peace.

BASIC SIGIL READING

1. **The Seeking**. What you are seeking by means of the query.

2. **The vision.** Your Expectation, the best possible form for what you are seeking

3. **What is looming;** what is just approaching; the immediate future

4. **What is preserved.** that which is protected or kept in reserve.

5. **What is coming into being.** The outcome of the Reading, that which has been set in motion.

6. **What helps.** What is assisting the outcome.

7. **What hinders.** What is inhibiting the outcome. Often requires reversing the oracular meaning of the Sigil. May signify expectations.

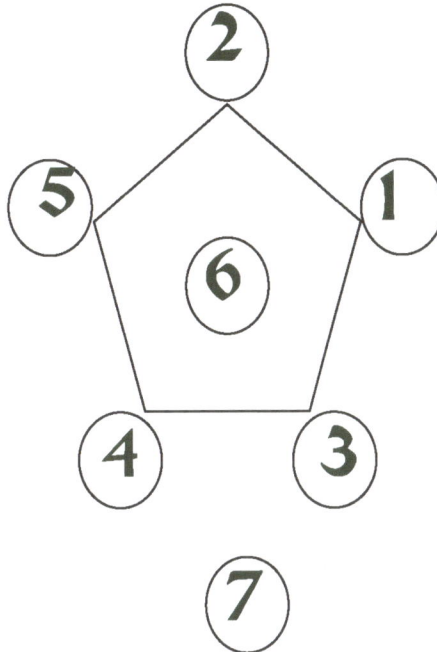

THREE SIGIL READING

1. **Present**.

2. **Past**.

3. **Future**

or

1. **Present**.

2. **expanding on 1.**.

3. **expanding on 1.** & 2

Oracle Charm

The following charm or any portion of it can be useful as a prelude to castng the Sigils:

Let leaves fall as they will,
Let Sigils speak and fill
The open cauldron of my question.
The streams of wisdom I do call,
The flow of Truth reveals them all,
The way is cast, The weave is spun
The Faery Speak,
The answers come.

Picture Credits

Pages 7-32
Sigils © 2013 by Coleston Brown.

Pages 6-36
Celtic Knot page runner © 1997 by
Jessie Skillen.

Page 7
Alchemical Rosicrucian illustration,1698. Image in Public Domain.

Page 8
Crannog-home built about 5000 years
ago in Loch Tay.Attribution: Christine
Westerback. Image licensed under the
Creative Commons Attribution-
ShareAlike 2.0 license.

Page 9
An ancient Cornish bank topped with
gorse and a hawthorn. Photo Courtesy geograph.org.uk

Page 10
Detail from the Mound, a painting by
Coleston Brown © 2007.

Page 11
The The Fairy Flag of Dunvegan and
Rob Mor's horn Photo Credit Roderick
Charles MacLeod ca. 1927. Image in
Public Domain.

Page 12
The Dome of Stars and The Sacred
Directions. Coleston Brown © 2011.

Page 13
Upper: The Haven Master and Faery
Child ©Jessie Skillen 2013; Lower:
The Faery Ship © Coleston Brown
2007

Page 14
Romano Celtic Bronze Mirror. Image
in Public Domain
Detail from The Watcher be A.E. (
George Russel),1907. Image courtesy
of National Museums Northern Ireland.

Page 15
A a Faery stick from County Sligo,
Ireland. Photo © 2013 Jessie Skillen

Page 16
A Sidhe ~ Painting by AE (George
Russell) Image in Public Domain.

Pages 17
Background from a Painting by AE
(George Russell) Public Domain: Right
Above: The Hand is an ancient im-
age,known from Palaeolithic times,
linking the Human to Presences in the
Land;
Right Below: the Faery Hand os
Friendship. Acrylic on wood by Jessie
Skillen 2010.

Page 18
Brigid painting, © 1998 Jessie Skillen.
inset Weyland's smithy, From the
Ardre Image Stone. Image in Public
Domain.

Page 19
Background, Dargle Waterfall.
Photo Credit, Sarah777 2003, Image
in Public Domain.
Inset Morigu, the faery Mare, Co
Sligo 3013. Image © Coleston Brown.

Page 20 Detail from Brigid painting
© Jessie Skillen, 1998.

Page 21
The Stream of Sigils by Coleston
Brown 2013

Page 22
The Utterer. Soft sculpture by Jessie
Skillen.

Page 23
The Spiral of Time. © 2013 Coleston
Brown.
Celtic Wheels Photo Credit PHGCOM ,
2009. Image in Public Domain.

Page 24
Aengus Og. Faery expressionist
painting © 2013 by Coleston Brown .
Acrylic, with a May tree thorn glued
to lower right ~used in creating parts

of the painting such as harp strings
and stone decoration.

Page 25
Bee on wood © 2013 by Jessie Skillen
&Rowan Tree, County Sligo, Ireland.

Page 26
The Star, painting © Coleston Brown
2008.

Page 27
Gundestrop Cauldron, Denmark.
150-0 BC. Image licensed under the
Creative Commons Attribution-
ShareAlike 2.0 license.

Page 28
The Hole Stone, Co Antrim, Northern
Ireland, 1994. Photo Credit Coleston
Brown 2010.
Hagstone. Photo Credit Jessie Skillen,
2013.

Page 29
The Mound, a painting by Coleston
Brown © 2007.

Page 30
An Altai/Scythian gold artefact,
Photo credit: Christine Asherah.

Page 31
Above, leaf shaped maze from Pim-
pern, Dorset.
inset: Frigg Weaving from Guerber, H.
A. (Hélène Adeline) (1909). Myths of
the Norsemen from the Eddas and
Sagas. London: Harrap. Image in the
Public Domain.

Page 32
Lightning flash, Unna Germany.
Photo credit: Rainer Knäpper,
Freenbsp;Art License (http://artlibre.o
rg/licence/lal/en).

Page 33: Sigil- Casting Diagrams by
Coleston Brown © 2013.

About The Author

Coleston Brown enjoys a simple life in the Irish countryside. He spends most of his free time quietly working on various projects designed to further the Faery-Human Covenant and the Magical Way.

www. magicalways.com

greenfirefoilios@gmail.com

Making or purchasing Sigils.

Sigils can be made by cutting 27 pieces of wooden doweling or (more difficult) tree branch. The Sigil signs are then drawn or painted on them. Occasionally, sets of sigils, handcrafted by Coleston Brown are for sale on www.magical ways .com. These are typically made of Rowan wood, but some sets are of Ash, Thorn or other hardwood. The Sigil sets come in handmade bags by Faery artist Jessie Skillen.

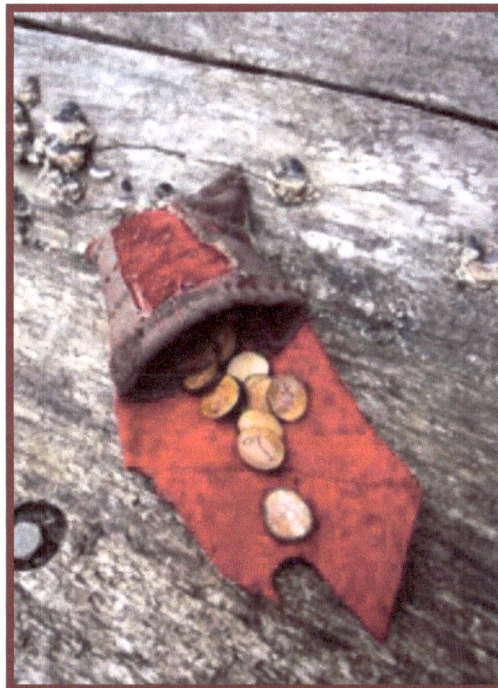

Ah	Bo'ah	Cu	Do'ah	Esh

Fir'eh	oG	Hu	aI	dJee'ah

aeiKou

eiL	Mu	Nu	O'ah	Phai

ohQ	Rai	Shay	Ti	U'ah

Vo	oWth	Xai	Yai	Zah	'thorn